ANIMAL ARTS AND CRAFTS

FARM
ANIMAL CRAFTS

Annalees Lim

 Gareth Stevens
PUBLISHING

CONTENTS

SAFETY PRECAUTIONS

We recommend adult supervision at all times while doing the activities in this book. Always be aware that craft materials may contain allergens, so check the packaging for allergens if there is a risk of an allergic reaction. Anyone with a known allergy must avoid these.

- Wear an apron and cover surfaces.
- Tie back long hair.
- Ask an adult for help with cutting.
- Check materials for allergens.

BEFORE YOU BEGIN

Do you know which animals live on a farm? Let's make some farm animals, and find out lots of fun facts about them along the way.

Follow the easy step-by-step instructions to start creating your own farm animal collection. When you have finished making an animal, you can also think about the kind of shelter it might live in.

A lot of the projects use paint and glue. Always cover surfaces with layers of old newspaper. Whenever you can, leave the project to dry before moving on to the next step. This avoids things getting stuck to each other or paint smudging.

Some of the equipment or materials needed to make these arts and crafts can be dangerous if they are not handled correctly. Please follow the instructions carefully and ask an adult to help you. Now get set to make your farm animal arts and crafts!

FLOCK OF SHEEP

Sheep live in large groups called flocks. Together, they graze grass on hillsides and in meadows. Make some hills for your own flock of sheep.

YOU WILL NEED:

- Glue stick
- Cotton balls
- Black, green, and blue card stock
- Brown felt-tip pen
- Scissors
- Pencil
- An adult to help you

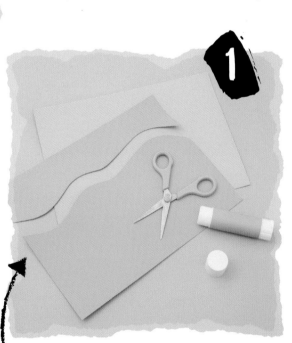

Ask an adult to help you with the cutting in this project. Cut a wavy shape from the green card stock. Stick it on the blue card stock, using the glue stick.

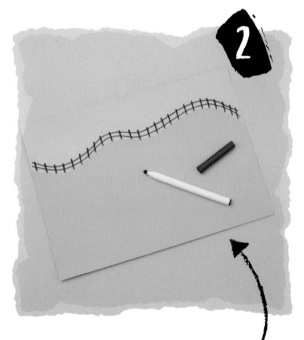

Now you have sky and hills. Use the brown felt-tip pen to add a fence.

Stick plenty of cotton balls onto the hills using the glue stick.

Use a pencil to draw lots of sheep heads and legs onto black card stock. Cut them out.

Glue the heads and legs onto the cotton ball sheep bodies.

DID YOU KNOW?

Farmers shear their sheep, or cut off their wool. This stops sheep from getting too hot during the summer.

SHEEP AND SHEEPDOG FACTS!

A baby sheep is called a lamb. A lamb drinks its mother's milk at first. Soon it starts nibbling grass as well.

If a lamb loses sight of its mother, it "baas" and she "baas" back. They know each other's calls.

Farmers train their border collies to obey words, calls, and whistles to help them with the sheep. It takes time and patience to train a border collie well.

Sheepdogs are any dogs that have been used to herd sheep. Border collies are one kind of sheepdog.

TRUSTY SHEEPDOG

Sheepdogs help farmers move flocks of sheep or herd a small group into a pen. Let's make a trusty sheepdog!

YOU WILL NEED:

- Two paper cups
- White, gray, and black paint
- Two paintbrushes
- Two sheets of black card stock
- Glue, tape
- Pencil
- Scissors
- Googly eyes
- Ruler
- Black felt-tip pen
- An adult to help you

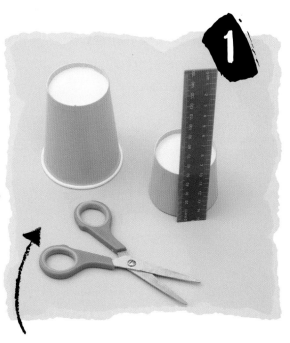

Ask an adult to help you cut one of the paper cups to be half the height of the whole cup.

Paint both cups black, gray, and white, to look like fur.

8

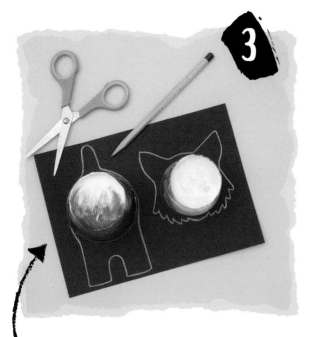

3

Glue both cups onto black card stock. Draw the outline of a dog's face around the shorter cup and its back legs and tail around the taller cup.

4

Ask an adult to help you cut out both shapes. Now draw the front legs on black card stock and cut them out too.

5

Glue the head and front legs to the dog's body. Cut out a nose from black card stock. Stick on the nose and googly eyes. Use a felt-tip pen to draw on a mouth.

DID YOU KNOW?

Your sheepdog is a border collie. Border collies are very smart, which is why people can train them as sheepdogs.

WOOLLY HIGHLAND COW

Highland cows are from
Scotland, where the weather
can get very cold. Make your
Highland cow really woolly,
so it stays warm!

YOU WILL NEED:

- Two sheets of orange card stock
- White card stock
- Green card stock
- Orange yarn
- Glue stick
- Scissors
- Pencil
- Tape
- Thin black marker
- An adult to help you

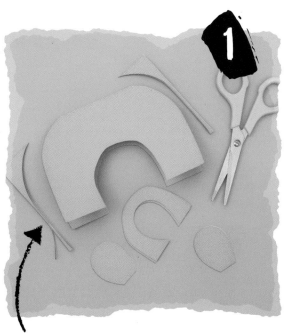

Ask an adult to help you with
the cutting in this project. Fold
a sheet of orange card stock in
half. Draw a C shape along the
open edge. Cut it out and cut
two ears from what's left.

Fold the other sheet of
orange card stock in half
and cut out a D shape
along the fold. Unfold the
card to form the head. Draw
on your cow's nostrils.

Open out the legs and fold the bottom of each to form hooves. Glue the hooves to the green card stock. Cut two slits into your cow's head.

Fold the white card stock in half and cut out a horn shape on the fold. Slide the tip of one horn through both slits to set the horns in place. Stick the head to the body and glue on ears.

Cut lengths of yarn to glue to the body of your cow and add shorter lengths for its forelock.

DID YOU KNOW?

It takes about three years for Highland cows to grow long, curved horns.

HIGHLAND COW FACTS!

Highland cows have two layers of hair: a warm undercoat and a longer overcoat. This protects them from rain and snow.

Highland cows make very good mothers.

PIG FACTS!

Pigs make lots of different noises when they talk to each other.

These pigs live outdoors. They are using their snouts to look for roots and insects to eat.

MUDDY PIGS

Pigs roll in mud to cool themselves down! You can make a mud bath for some modeling clay pigs.

Fill the flowerpot tray with soil and press down firmly. Now wash your hands.

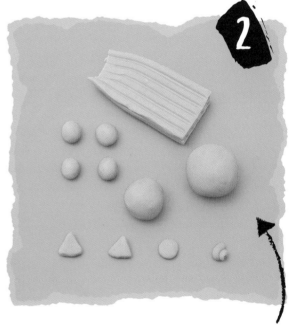

Use pink modeling clay to form a large ball, a medium-sized ball, four small balls, two small triangles, a small squished ball, and a snake shape that you need to curl up to be your pig's tail.

Press all the shapes together to create a pig. Make another set of shapes to form a sitting pig.

Use black modeling clay to form your pigs' eyes. Use white modeling clay to make nostrils.

To make a pig that looks like it is diving into the mud, make a large ball, two small balls, and a curly tail and press them together. Place all your pigs in the soil tray.

DID YOU KNOW?

Pigs are very smart! Some people say they are smarter than any other kind of farm animal or pet.

QUILLED CHICK

Fluffy chicks live in barns and farmyards. Make your own yellow chick using quilled paper!

YOU WILL NEED:

- Yellow, orange, and black quilling paper or shredded paper
- Glue stick
- Green card stock
- Yellow card stock
- An adult to help you

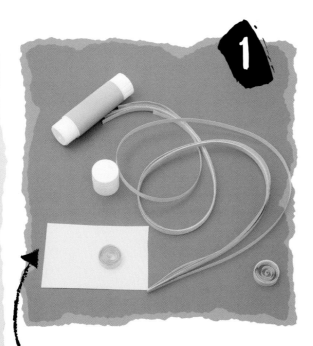

Take a yellow paper strip. Roll it into a loose coil and glue the end in place. Stick the coil onto yellow card stock. This is the chick's head. Make a slightly larger coil to form the body.

Make two smaller yellow coils. Pinch one end of each to form teardrop shapes. Stick them to the sides of the body to make the wings.

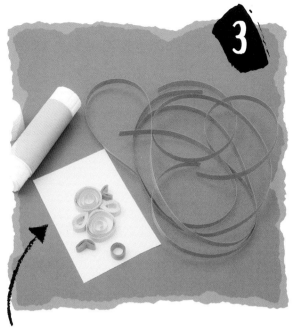

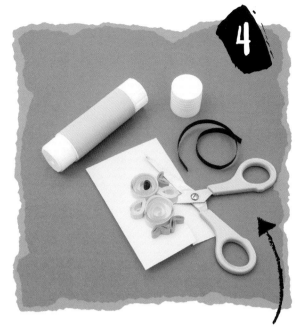

Make three orange coils. Flatten them and fold them into V shapes. Stick two to the body to make feet and use one to make the beak.

Make a small, tight black coil. Stick it into the head to make an eye. Ask an adult to cut around the chick.

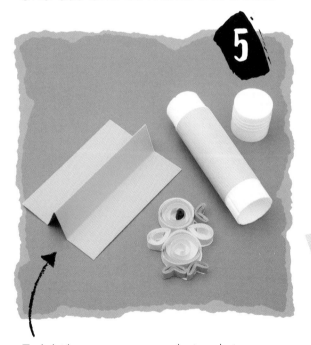

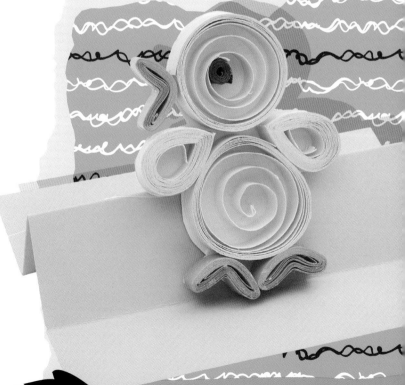

Fold the green card stock to create a V shape in the center. Glue the back of the quilled chick to the card stock.

DID YOU KNOW?

Chicks are very small when they hatch. You could hold one in your hand!

HORSE IN A STABLE

Some farmers keep horses because they like riding them, or they use them to herd cattle. Make your model horse a stable to sleep in.

Use the ruler and pencil to mark the center of the dark brown card stock. Fold each side into the center. Make a firm crease along each fold.

Use the felt-tip pen to draw lines onto the front of the card flaps. These will make the wooden stable doors for your horse.

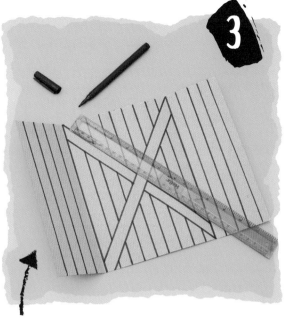

Open up the stable doors. Use the felt-tip pen to draw the inside of the stable.

Draw the outline of a horse's head and neck onto the light brown card stock. Ask an adult to help cut them out.

Cut both stable doors to create two small flaps at the bottom and two big flaps at the top. Stick your horse's neck to the stable wall. Fold over the bottom flaps and glue on its head. Stick on the googly eyes.

DID YOU KNOW?

Farmers used to use horses to pull carts, plows, and other farm equipment.

19

GOAT SOCK PUPPET

Goats are clever animals. They can learn their name and will come when you call them. You can teach this goat sock puppet even more tricks!

Ask an adult to cut the pipe cleaner in half. Then cut out four long triangles from dark brown felt. They should be 0.5 inch (1.2 cm) shorter than the pipe cleaners.

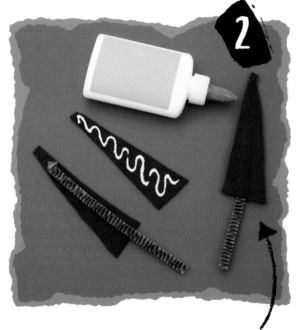

Glue a pipe cleaner between two felt triangles, leaving a bit of pipe cleaner sticking out at the bottom. Repeat, so that you have two sets. Leave to dry.

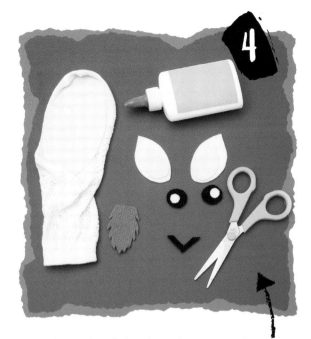

Cut an oval shape from pink felt to fit the sole of the sock. Glue the pink circle to the sole to make the mouth of your goat.

Using the black, white, pink, and brown felt, cut out your goat's ears, eyes, nose, and a little beard. Stick them all onto the sock using fabric glue.

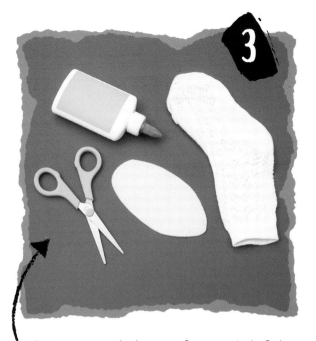

Twist the felt triangles and the pipe cleaners to make the horns. Stick the pipe cleaner ends into the goat's head and bend them to keep them in place.

DID YOU KNOW?

Female goats are called nanny goats, male goats are called billy goats, and baby goats are called kids!

GOAT FACTS!

Farmers around the world milk goats. The milk is sold for drinking or made into goat cheese.

Goats are clever and curious.

DONKEY FACTS!

Donkeys can live to over 40 years of age! Their large ears help them hear donkey calls from far away.

A baby donkey is called a foal. It can stand up 30 minutes after it is born.

DONKEY BEANBAG

Donkeys like living together in herds. They become close friends with other donkeys or horses in their field. Have fun making this donkey beanbag.

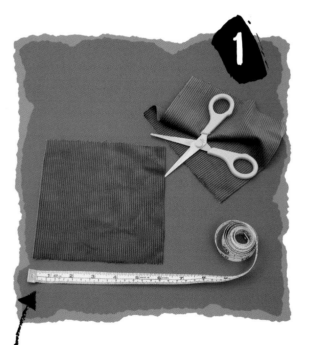

Ask an adult to help you cut out two squares of blue corduroy fabric that are 6 x 6 inches (15 x 15 cm).

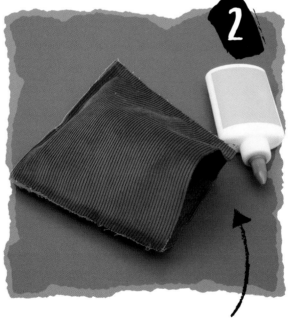

Glue the edges of the squares together to form seams, leaving one end open. Wait until the glue has dried before moving on to the next step.

Fill the bag with rice. Pull the opposing seams together and glue them, so that you have a triangular beanbag.

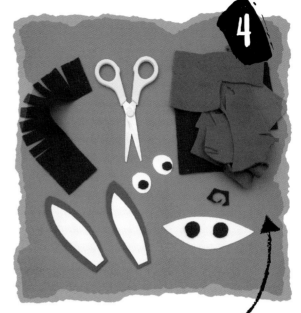

Ask an adult to help you cut out shapes from the felt to make a nose, ears, mane, and eyes.

Glue all the shapes onto your donkey's head and leave it to dry.

DID YOU KNOW?

A male donkey is called a jack, and a female donkey is called a jenny!

SHELL GOOSE

Geese like to live in groups, called gaggles. Use lots of seashells of different sizes to make your own gaggle of geese!

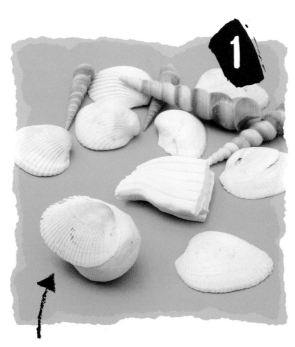

Roll a piece of modeling clay into a ball. Press a fan shell into each side to make the wings of your goose.

Press a spiral shell into the modeling clay in between the two shell wings. This will form the neck of your goose.

Form a piece of clay into a teardrop shape and press it onto the top of the shell neck to give your goose a head.

Ask an adult to help you use scissors to cut into the head to form the beak.

Paint the beak orange. Press googly eyes onto each side of your goose's head.

DID YOU KNOW?

Geese are good at guarding a farm. They honk loudly and will even chase people away!

GOOSE FACTS!

Geese have webbed feet for swimming but spend most of their time on land. They use their beaks to eat grass and other plants.

Baby geese are called goslings.

DUCK FACTS!

Unlike many kinds of birds, ducklings can walk and swim from the start. They will follow their mother wherever she leads them.

A mother duck keeps her ducklings safe, shows them what is good to eat, and keeps them warm at night.

DUCK POND

Baby ducks are called ducklings. Make a pond for your yellow ducklings to swim on.

YOU WILL NEED:

- Ziplock bag
- Blue hair gel
- Yellow and orange foam sheets
- Scissors and spoon
- Wide tape
- Craft glue
- Dark green, light green, and blue card stock
- Googly eyes
- An adult to help you

1

Ask an adult to help you with the cutting out. Cut pieces of light green and blue card stock the width of the ziplock bag. Cut a D shape out of the light green card stock.

2

Cut three duckling shapes and three wings out of the yellow foam and three beaks from the orange foam. Glue a beak, a wing, and a googly eye to each duckling.

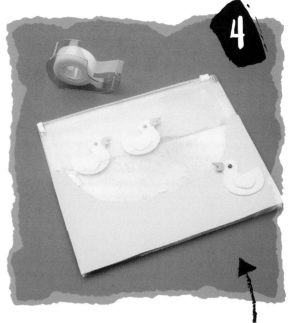

Stick the green card stock to the front of the bag and the blue card stock to the back. Spoon some blue hair gel into the bag to act as water.

Place your foam ducklings inside the bag, swimming on the hair gel. Zip the bag and seal it with tape.

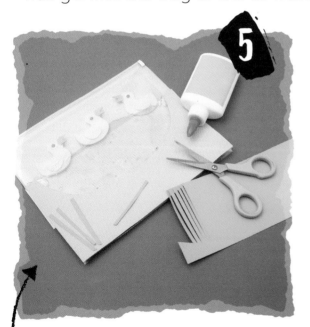

Decorate the edge of the pond with reeds made from dark green card stock.

DID YOU KNOW?

Wild ducks live on ponds, rivers, lakes, and the ocean. They all have waterproof feathers.

GLOSSARY

graze eat grass

hatch come out of an egg

herd make a group of animals move along, or the name for a group of animals, such as cows

pen fencing around a small area

snout long nose of an animal

trusty faithful and reliable

webbed toes connected by skin to aid swimming

INDEX

Please visit our website, www.garethstevens.com. For a free color catalog of all our high-quality books, call toll free 1-800-542-2595 or fax 1-877-542-2596.

Published in 2025 by **Gareth Stevens Publishing** 2544 Clinton St. Buffalo, NY 14224

First published in Great Britain in 2022 by Wayland

Copyright © Hodder and Stoughton, 2022 Wayland

Acknowledgements:
Shutterstock: Shaun Barr 7b; Peter Betts 7t; Defotoberg 12; Geza Farkas 23; Lois GoBe 13b; Haidamac 28; Juice Flair 6; William Kuhl Photographs 13t; Alexander Paramonov 29; Smereka 22.

Every effort has been made to clear copyright. Should there be any inadvertent omission please apply to the publisher for rectification.

Cataloging-in-Publication Data
Names: Lim, Annalees.
Title: Farm animal crafts / Annalees Lim.
Description: New York : Gareth Stevens Publishing, 2025. | Series: Animal arts and crafts | Includes glossary and index.
Identifiers: ISBN 9781538294383 (pbk.) | ISBN 9781538294390 (library bound) | ISBN 9781538294406 (ebook)
Subjects: LCSH: Handicraft--Juvenile literature. | Animals in art--Juvenile literature. | Domestic animals in art--Juvenile literature.
Classification: LCC TT160.L56 2025 | DDC 745.5--dc23

Editor, and author of the fact pages: Sarah Ridley
Design: Collaborate
Craft photography: Simon Pask, N1 Studios